C000095128

THE UNQUIET

First published in 2019
by Offord Road Books

www.offordroadbooks.co.uk

Typeset by Offord Road Books
Printed in the UK by Palace Printers

All rights reserved © L. Kiew, 2019

The right of L. Kiew to be identified as author
of this work is asserted in accordance with Section 77
of the Copyrights, Designs and Patents Act 1988

ISBN 978–1–999–93047–9

1 3 5 7 9 10 8 6 4 2

The Unquiet

L. KIEW

Swallow

Grammars gather on powerlines.
Verbs twitter in the mangifera.
I roost in humid shade,
overeating from the dictionary –
nouns sticky as langsat,
a kilo of adjuncts, a kati of adverbs.

    uà ài: gāt lèu dă: jek dă uę
orotund   nullibiety   opaque
smeasling   desuetude   spoilage
    uà ài: gāt lèu dă: jek dă uę
minatory   plangent   deliquesce
lutulent   sportive   grackle

The words I swallow become
feathers poking through my skin.
I am fledging for the migration.
A window yawns,
a line of lipstick
palms reddening the horizon.

Bridge

We accrete buttressing
around the hips in this family
as we approach our fifties;
our tendons lose their flex
over the architecture of bone
and tensioned, become cables.

It takes increasing effort
to invert and scratch
our toes, to squat down,
to sit cross-legged –

finally it's impossible
to recline on the ground.

We come to a standstill.
Our vertebrae settle as stones.

With our siblings, the spandrels,
we hold up the long
span across which our children
race their cars towards Canaan.

Haunts

I

Lạomà believes the dead
cling to their possessions.
My dress is red shantung;
its last occupant is
heartbroken and tugging
on my hem.

The widower holds me
at arms' length, cold and stiff.
I waltz around, around.
When I sink down, a white hand
strokes my feet, smearing black
blood over my cracked heels.

II

Ah Jek visited that night,
breath stinking of arak.
Those black brogues. Give them back.

Five daughters, many school shoes.
There wasn't enough
money to buy brand-new.

Shoes taken off, gather
dust and ash. Ah Jek wears
loafers, a paper suit.

III

In his office of black scrolls
Yama reads out the sentence.
          I repudiate; not me.
I dispute until dawn.

Sticky rice I'll harvest next
time.   His ink-stained index traces
down the night's ledger and
          I am slammed awake.
Next door someone is crying.

Open fingers, palms up.
In the first hand, red silk
cord, a thin white braid of hair;
in the second, an egg.

Francesca

who stood
ready at one o'clock

with fried rice on a plate
and Yeo's tomato ketchup

who makes sweet
and sour pork better than anyone

who taught me
how to peel prawns and boil

the shells to inhibit their smell and
civets from coming to the backyard

who tends
the avocado tree, who picks its fruit

who showed me chicken feathers
snakeskin feet, choppered its head

draining rich ruby into
a bowl, coagulating

who walks to church
daily, strong as bamboo

as persistent, who lives
on the hill

Pitched in

kangbāng covered in dust
a worn shirt on the line
with no one to fill it

Father at the door
I refused twelve
this was all that was left

kiaogià empty rice bowls
anguish springs like bamboo
on steep slopes

duạ jò duạ, sòi jò sòi
to marry a tiger
sacrifice that ox-hearted nature

jáobhọlou drunk home
his chickenhead zooming
on my throat

dragging steps
msa:msĭ
the water is dark

The Catch

When he brought that stinky parcel
of catfish home from the market,
Mother-in-law turned her eyes away
like swifts skimming across water.

My heart was an empty
house with its red door swinging wide.
I held our little fish
safe from the monsoon, the gossip

the storm clouds hurled and smashed papayas
against the shutters.
It's impossible to wash the face of
our house clean.

Learning to be mixi

I

It was so panas
but aircon in airport
bite like cat.
Mother wave goodbye at gate
and
I was buckled in, and taken off
to England, the boarding school
(not like Enid Blyton, not at all) and
Cambridge, the colleges,
the backs and the hate,
suppressing the suffix-lah,
being proper and nice, cutting
my tongue with that ice.

II

Ah Kong love learning-lah,
every day
reading *Sin Chew Jit Poh*,
give his grandchildren all good
name: Hsueh Hui, Hsueh Zi,

call my brother lazy worm
for not reading book
but
when we came home

we left the chill,
Shakespeare at passport control,
filled our ears with warm tones,
jiat hò a bhuę?

When I took my Scots partner home
speaking proper English, he asked
'Honey, di'ye ken ye jest switched
tongues mid-sentence.'
Dialect like a blush licked
my face, campur–campur
speech bursting the ice wall,
jǫpuēt: puēt uę.

The boy I wasn't

carries the family name like a Langyao vase
sweeps the graves and burns altar incense
offers roast duck and arak at Ch'ing Ming

little Emperor, I resented you
as an ox resents mire
paralysed with loneliness

every New Year I send photos of you
in red envelopes to Lạomà
she asks after your apple-faced babies

no one calls me outside
water drips from mossed rock
bats nibble at the darkness

this girl becomes a sea swallow
my spit-cup nest high up the cave wall
fledging above the scent of waves

Foreign language syndrome

That bumper brutal to the skull
knocked me back
years

speaking
Hokkien learnt in the playground
counting the rope turns
chit, nng, sa, sì, go, lák
Di simmi mia?

healing
synapses pull home
sharing out rambutans with brother
jēk, nó, sa, sĭ, ngóu, làk
Chiá: meụng lèu miạ mītgāi?

English bleeds
over the ground
onto my tongue

13

Speech

Ah Ba speak red: liddat tone
of voice sure salah wan.
Rojak-say okay wan. She learn
from school proper taupau can.
At home no need to paiseh.

At boarding school, it was strange
to feel so constantly – other.
Where are you from? What's your accent?
Diam, diam or they come laugh,
laugh you lah, bò-ĕng lah.

Home, in the doorway,
I hear: ah, my flat ā springs from
my Mother's granite cubes
of clipped clarity splashing into
the thick earth of Ah Ba's voice.

And I let my words landslide,
ferrous, carrying both stone chips,
rice and tapioca roots.
I dig down, ah, I speak lah,
pearl and pebble, new shoots.

Dinner

In Tesco I stand in front of frozen meat.
A flitch of bacon was awarded to another
couple on Whit Monday. We fry up fast

and casual. Don't wait up, don't even try,
lie down. You cold cut sandwiches
on Saturdays. The first litmus turns red,

the second deficient pink. We keep on trying.
I expect a bivalve, a blue line. To knuckle
under is to submit. The table's underside

is a struggle. My knuckles are raw. Why don't
you answer? The barber's pole represents
the staff gripped in venesection. We couldn't

stop bleeding. Do you hear that? Dripping.
Though I love you, I wipe the bowl. The sink's red.
Beetroot tops. Chopped rind. A joint defrosting.

Balik kampung

When I return I want
it to be this

Father in a sarong and t-shirt
walking the five-foot way
calling on shopkeepers
in his mouthful of dialects
and the evening shopping done
reaching for my sticky hand
and crossing to our Ford Escort

But I look back
over my shoulder

A child stands at the verge
staring at the rush hour traffic
with Proton Sagas and lorries
in an unending rattling roar
and there is no one left to
take her anxious hand

Immersion Learning

Water pervades, flowing into
depression, between cracks
into aquifers. My daughter looks
at silt left behind after the flood,
shells, feathers, a plastic egg
docked against damp twigs,

then asks me why at the end
of a work meeting Paul swivelled
towards her and spouted,
'At least you learnt something.'
Frequent droplets drill a hole
through stone. But I understand.

You've learnt some men believe
they have the voice of storms,
downdraughts of revelation.
Daughter, you don't have to
imbibe. Truth puts mud in
water. You have riparian rights

and Daughter, I was flat skin
until a saltwater incursion
inflated my lungs, gave me
the waves' shingled roar.
To speak against the current
is to swim wild. Don't sink

into silence. Wind dulls down.
Tide turns and returns.
Buoyancy is also your birthright
by the moon's wet slap.
Kicking was your first conversation.
You are a strong swimmer.

Cryptography

what I am saying is
certain words go deep

glabrous
catawampous
nescience

like a forgotten cellar
under the house of your childhood

and no telling
what you will
find

among the dusty
glottals on one page
the codes on the other

understanding comes sometimes
and only sometimes clear

legible
as frost's annotations
on the morning's pane

Bridled

Days lashed together, long strips
around my body, giftwrapped.
You say trust me. You excel
at rope work. Uà tia: m̥ bak.

Tell me again. With macramé,
create mats, rings and truss.
Knotting is a matter of life and
death, especially among sailors.

Cords rig our armchairs,
footstools and overhead lights.
Suspended, your hands circle.
I stutter. Dà: lại dà: keu.

My tongue frays. The hitch slips.
I kick and kick. Lèu m̥ tia.
Yokes transmit tension.
You whisper. The harness holds.

Ask me

some time
when the smoke is
a scrim across the sky.

Ask me when dusk
falls with hail
peppering the fields,

when the wind
harries dry leaves
from the canopy.

No matter what salt
seasons the hour, ask me.
The answer will be yes.

Afterlife

Jáobhọlọu, she'd had to go,
steerage rat on the iron boat
from Swatow; she'd refused again
and again to bind her feet.

Stubbornness landed her,
an old husband, nanyang,
their dry goods store, years
raising two sons, one not hers,
six daughters, grandchildren,
bò-ĕng till the very last day.

★★★

To hold her hand is to hold iron.
Lạomà's palms are restless.
She forges a railroad from room to room.
Stationed she makes pomelos flower.
The peeled segments are fragrant.
Outside orchids overflow pots.

When Niutāo and Bhèming call,
she escapes under the back door
along the yellow wall, scurrying
grey and fast into the lalang –

Winter sea

even this far inland
we hear the grinding
rattling shingle

its teeth clenched
tears bitten back

we approach the sea
cold
to the imploring moon

and the sight of it shocks us
cutting the muscle
open along the inside of our shell

because the light scatters
that stretch of water
into indifferent night

and the surf withdraws
with a shrug
bearing the ashes

Lassaba

if I come to visit   calling her name
from the other side of the locked gate
                would she whisper back
while unhooking the rusted padlock

with the lightest of touches   no more
than a moth's white sweep on my arm
                    would she usher me in

if I come   and stay the night
my parents on expedition upriver
                    would she remain by me

    would her hand stop on my ankle
as a cloud pauses over the moon
against a dim bulb   paper wings
filling the hall with their shadows

Mediums

in dreams I openmouth
sensekelp sidelopped
water even more complicating

okay lah, you like that say
talk cheekblow
tongueburr you blur what!

I sacrifice puggytears
tosswords
joss the waves

like that, selamat
also, don't know how to do
sense tidak melekat

I row learnings
chòukŏu guĭ lipstrike
earlicked straits

who say our speak is teruk?
you clear too
some canals not open

sound carrycross water
brothersistercousins joyneed
we unclose, belong

cincai, like that lah
meaning bocor
sometimes no need words, listen

Acknowledgements

I am grateful to the editors of the following publications in which some of these poems or versions of them first appeared: *Dreamcatcher, Haverthorn, Losslit, Obsessed with Pipework, Tears in the Fence* and *The Scores*. I am also grateful to the Poetry School, for featuring some poems on their website. 'Francesca' was chosen as a runner-up in the Bi'an Awards 2019.

My thanks also to Patience Agbabi, Louise Anne Buchler, Lewis Buxton, David Caddy, Kayo Chingonyi, Miriam Gamble, Joanna Ingham, Hannah Lowe, Helena Nelson, and my fellow TOAST poets, all of whom have given me inspiration and feedback as I worked towards this pamphlet.

Special thanks to Mike Weston for his continuing support and love, Martha Sprackland and everyone at Offord Road Books for their generosity, and to Jennifer Schamotta for the cover.